Secret Hiding Places

(for Clever Kids)

Mark Shulman

Sterling Publishing Co., Inc.
New York

SECRET HIDING PLACES
(for Clever Kids)

Author **Mark Shulman**
Book Designer **Madeleine Budnick**
Illustrator **Annie Galvin**
Creative Directors **Hallie Warshaw**
and **Mark Shulman**

Created by

Ŏrange Avenue

Making Creative Products for Growing Minds

San Francisco • New York

Library of Congress Cataloging-in-Publication Data Available

10 9 8 7 6 5 4 3 2 1

Published by Sterling Publishing Company, Inc.
387 Park Avenue South, New York, NY 10016

© 2001 Mark Shulman
Illustrations © 2001 Annie Galvin

Created and produced by Orange Avenue, Inc.
275 Fifth Street, San Francisco, CA 94103, USA
www.orangeavenue.com

Distributed in Canada by Sterling Publishing Co., Inc.
c/o Canadian Manda Group, One Atlantic Avenue, Suite 105
Toronto, Ontario, Canada M6K 3E7

Distributed in Great Britain and Europe by Chris Lloyd
463 Ashley Road, Parkstone, Poole, Dorset BH14 0AX, England

Distributed in Australia by Capricorn Link (Australia) Pty Ltd.
P.O. Box 6651, Baulkham Hills, Business Centre NSW 2153, Australia

Printed in China
All rights reserved
Sterling ISBN 0-8069-6853-2

**For Kara and Esther,
who always know when I'm hiding something.**

ACKNOWLEDGMENTS:

Secret Hiding Places Covert Testing Team: Brendan Finn (Team Leader), Daniel Gomez, Andrew Finn, Joseph Gomez, Charlie Gomez, Nathan Boyar, and the staff and students at Windermere Boulevard School.

Thanks to Charles Nurnberg, Frances Gilbert, Hallie Warshaw, Madeleine Budnick, Annie Galvin, Robyn Brode, Tanya Napier, Marcio Baggio, and Robert Warshaw for helping make this book. Thanks to Bill & Rachel Finn and Mary Lavin for everything, including the kids. Thanks to Café Aroma, Coffee Bean Café, and Spot Coffee in Buffalo for hiding me when I needed to write. And thanks to my sisters, Sharon, Barbara, and Ellie, for all the years of practice. It was under the bottom shelf in the linen closet.

ABOUT THE AUTHOR

Mark Shulman writes for children and adults.

He was an early reader, an uncle at eight years old, a camp counselor, a radio newscaster, a New York City tour guide, and an advertising creative director before writing this book. He is the youngest of five children, and he grew up reading Sherlock Holmes and Dashiell Hammett in an old house full of corners.

Mark graduated from East High School in Rochester, NY, and the University of Buffalo. He and his wife Kara live in New York.

WHAT HAVE YOU GOT TO HIDE?

Where do you keep your diary? Your letters and notes? Your valuables? And all the things you never want to lose?

You can keep your favorite items safe **without** a safe, or even a lock. Open your eyes to boring little places where nobody looks. Build fake walls and other secret vaults. Leave innocent, stray clues that guide your friends to your special coded maps, and more.

You'll discover secret hiding places at home, at school, and in-between. And you'll find **extra** secret hiding places at

www.SecretHidingPlaces.com

But don't forget where you hid this book. Now hide it!

THE TWELVE LAWS
OF HIDING STUFF

1. THE LAW OF LEAVE IT ALONE

Hide it once, hide it well, and fight the urge to go back. Attracting too much attention will leave clues and give away the game. Out of sight, out of mind.

2. THE LAW OF FEWER FOOTPRINTS

Your hiding places shouldn't be busy places. Pick areas that people don't use all the time, or places where they won't usually stop. Hiding places often get discovered on cleaning day.

3. THE LAW OF IGNORE ME

Make sure the area around your hiding place looks normal and boring. And don't make your vault too tricky or complex. Cleverness sometimes backfires, while simple places get ignored.

4. THE LAW OF WISE PLANNING

Before you hide it, know how often you'll want it. Some tricky hiding places are better for the long term. Also have a few quick places ready for instant access.

5. THE LAW OF MIX-IT-UP

Don't use only one kind of hiding place. People who do are easy to figure out. Also, be sure to switch places around now and then, just to be safe.

6. THE LAW OF OPEN EYES

New hiding places spring up all the time. Stay on the lookout, then move quickly and quietly. Scout the place a bit first. Make sure no one's focused on it, and that it isn't about to be sold, moved, or trashed.

7. THE LAW OF PLAYING SAFE

Too many hiding places at once are hard to manage. They're also easier for others to find. Keep it under control.

8. THE LAW OF TREASURE ISLAND

Make coded treasure maps and update them when you need to. Make your code easy to remember and use. Keep your maps in special map-hiding places.

9. THE LAW OF SECRETS

Try to avoid telling other people about your secret hiding places. You may feel clever, but once the secret is out, you can't get it back. If you do show off your places, only show a few of them.

10. THE LAW OF NATURE

Food goes bad quickly. Avoid hiding anything except hard candy like lollipops. Even then, think about the awful things heat and time can do to food. Make only one hiding place for that candy, and keep it current.

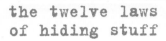

11. THE LAW OF FAIR PLAY

Use your new powers for good. Don't hide other people's things from them. There's honor among hiders.

12. THE MASTER LAW

Never hide anything that will get you into trouble.

Stay away from dangerous and stupid things. It's not fun to get hurt or to hurt other people. You know you'll get caught—and punished. Why mess up your life when you're just a kid? Be smart. Hiding is really about creative thinking, making things, and having fun.

Now go have fun!

SECRET GLOSSARY

Secret hiding places have their own special language. These are some of the official terms.

CACHE (sounds like "cash") As a noun, a cache is whatever item(s) you've hidden. As a verb, it means to hide. Examples: I keep a cache of comic books behind a fake wall. I cached them there yesterday.

CAMOUFLAGE (KAM-uh-flawzh) As a verb, it means to decorate something so it blends into its environment. As a noun, it's whatever helps something hide. Examples: I camouflaged the box by covering it with a sweater. I could also have used my jacket as camouflage.

DECOY (DEE-koy) Noun: something used to fool, lure, or draw attention toward one thing or away from another. Example: The cardboard box says "trading cards," but it's just a decoy. Actually, I hide my trading cards in a magazine.

DROP As a noun, the place where a message or item has been left or hidden. As a verb, agents also call this "making a drop." Examples: I left the note in the usual drop. I made the drop this morning.

LANDMARK Noun: An obvious (and hopefully permanent) object used to help you hide or find something. Example: I'll hide the box under the third streetlight from the corner. That streetlight will be the landmark.

PARTNER Noun or verb: A person you team up with to create codes, send messages, build vaults, and make hiding places. When you do this, you are partnering together.

SURVEILLANCE (sur-VAY-lints) Noun: Keeping close watch over something or someone.

VAULT Noun: Any compartment for keeping valuables safe. In this book, the vaults are the contraptions you create yourself.

Bedroom Chambers

**If you're like most of us, your bedroom is your castle.
And nothing makes your castle more fun
than the secrets inside it. The formula is simple:
Closed Door = Privacy = Creativity.**

IN THE CLOSET:

POCKET PACKS:

The clothes in your closet are filled with pockets. Why keep them empty? During the warm months, your winter coat's pockets and sleeves are perfect for the job.

HANGER UPPER:

Use a coat hanger as a decoy. Hang a refillable bag from the hanger, then put your clothes over it. Pants are especially good for this.

FEET FEAT:

Drop something small in a shoe and shake it toward the toe. Big items need boots. Put the shoes back when you're done. Don't be too neat, if that's not your style. If you keep shoes in a shoebox, you can hide stuff under the tissue, too.

HAT TRICK:

Hide a secret in a baseball cap. Then hang the cap from a hook. Or tape something inside a hat and put the hat out of reach.

ON A SHELF:

CAN YOU CD HIDING PLACE?

Cards and money hide well in the front booklets of CD cases. Or go deluxe and hide it inside the back half. First remove the plastic cover by gently pushing the top hinge away with your thumb. (Don't break it!)

Now you've just got the back half that holds the CD. At the top corner, work your thumb between the top tray and the clear plastic back. Gently separate and remove the tray. Between the tray and the paper tucked behind it, you can hide whatever fits, which isn't much. Putting it all back together is just common sense: Don't force it, and make sure the sides of the printed paper are in place before snapping it shut. Put one hinge from the cover into place, then gently pull the other one over until it locks in.

SHELF AWARENESS:

Books in a bookcase don't always reach all the way to the back. Put those books on a high shelf, where it's hard to see what's behind them, and pull each book all the way to the edge. The space between the books and the wall defines what you can hide back there. Removing a few books works just like a door.

BOOK IT:

Dollar bills, paper, and cards will fit inside the pages of a book if you only hide a few. Spread them throughout the book, making sure the edges don't show. If you have a hardback book with a paper jacket over

it, remove the jacket and tape your treasure onto the hard cover. To learn how to cut a hiding place **into** an unwanted book, turn to page 62.

PICTURE THIS:

Do you keep your photos in clear plastic sleeves, back to back in a photo album? Think about how easy it would be to hide trading cards between them. People can even browse your photos without finding out!

ARE YOU GAME?

Board games look so innocent...and hide so much. They're big, they're filled with noisy stuff, and they just sit there. Pick a game you don't really play anymore.

THE VIDEO GAME:

Take a regular cardboard videocassette box and stuff it with your stuff. Write the name of a movie nobody likes, or even make up your own movie name. Then put the box in the pile with the rest of them. If you're feeling really creative, make the Video Vault on page 72.

IN A DRAWER:

USE SOME PULL:

They may look inside a drawer, but behind it? Flat items can be taped there, or tucked into taped-on envelopes. Make sure the drawer closes naturally. On lower drawers, tape papers under the bottom, but don't let them get in the way of the drawer. If what you're hiding is really flat, pull out the top drawer and tape it snugly under the bottom.

THE MESS ADVANTAGE:

Papers and money tucked into old magazines or inside old homework hide beautifully among the junk.

SOCK IT TO THEM:

If your family usually rolls clean socks into balls, set aside a special pair in the drawer. Hide something in the toe of one sock and roll them both back up. If you actually need to wear the socks, move the item or walk funny.

AROUND THE ROOM:

TISSUE BOXING:

Half-full boxes of facial tissue make a very easy hide. Pinch the tissues in the middle and lift them all out in one or two groups. Don't take too many at once or you'll make a mess. Lay something inside the box bottom, and

make sure it doesn't move around. Lay the tissues flat and replace them in the same clumps you pulled out, but not pinched. Don't sneeze too often! If you do, add tissues from another box before your secret's out.

BATTERY POWER:

Inside your boom box, your flashlight, and your electronic toys, you'll find a perfect hiding place—the battery compartment. But be careful: **DON'T PLUG ANYTHING IN** and **DON'T HIDE ANY METAL IN THERE.** Metal can conduct electricity, shock you, or start a fire. Like they say at the supermarket, paper or plastic.

TOY STORY:

Speaking of old toys, take a look at some of yours. Can you tuck things inside without breaking anything? It's better to give away toys you don't want than ruin them, so be careful while you're being clever. Then put the toys away where toys belong.

CORD TRICKS:

Tape a foot-long piece of string to a bag or envelope. Put the other end of the string under a lamp that's sitting on a dresser or desk. Run the string along the lamp cord and dangle the envelope between the furniture and the wall. A simple pull of the string is all you need.

GET FRAMED:

There are too many kinds of picture frames to explain here, but this idea isn't rocket science. Only use small, stand-up frames for regular photos. No wall frames, and stay away from the important pictures that can't be replaced. Whatever you do, do it gently, since glass is usually involved. The thing you're hiding has to fit between the photo and the cardboard behind it. Make sure you can't see what you've hidden. And wipe off your fingerprints...

TABLE TOPPER:

If you can reach beneath a table, you can tape an envelope or pouch there. Try to match the table's color. Slide your hand underneath for a fast hide and a fast retrieve. Try to pick a table in a quiet corner. The lower, the better.

SHADY MOVE:

Some rooms have roll-up window shades. Gently pull one down until the window is covered. Tape small, flat, flexible paper up near the top. Then give a small tug at the bottom. Don't let it snap back up—guide it, don't wreck it. This is where the spies in movies hide their maps.

IT'S CURTAINS:

If your room has curtains, carefully examine how they connect to the rod. Maybe you can hang something small and soft, like a drawstring bag, along the top in the folds of the curtain. Hook the bag to one of the hooks with a twist-tie, and make sure the curtains open and close easily. Go outside to see if anything's exposed, and watch for bulges inside, too.

BEDROOM PLACES TO AVOID:
- In your dresser among the clothes
- Between your mattress protector and the mattress
- Under the bed
- Under seat cushions
- Where vacuums go

COMPUTE THIS:

Hide little things under your computer keyboard...or mousepad. But be gentle. Don't put anything near the computer or printer—the loose spaces help ventilation and avoid overheating.

POSTER HOST:

If you're allowed to tape or tack posters to your wall, pay attention. You can hide maps and secret documents on the wall behind your art. If you use tape, put a piece of clear tape on the wall directly under the place your poster connects to the wall. Put another piece on the bottom corners of your poster. Because the top tape sticks to the bottom tape and not the wall, it can be removed and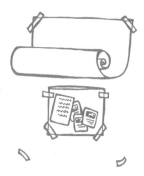
replaced more easily. If you use push pins, be careful not to make too big a hole in the wall, or the pins will fall out. Tape works better.

CAN IT:

If you're the one who empties the trash, and you use trash bags, good news. There's a quick hide right under your nose—so to speak—in the space between the bag and the bottom of the can. Don't expect anything here to last long, or smell good either. In and out.

Household Hideouts

You're not alone at home. Other people are living in the living room, bathing in the bathroom, and kitching in the kitchen. So you've got to be extra clever, and extra careful.

OUT-OF-THE-WAY PLACES:

LUG THE LUGGAGE:

Most of the time, suitcases and trunks do nothing but fill up closets and other forgettable places. But keep up with the family travel schedule, or else your secret stuff might end up going far, far away.

BRIGHT IDEA:

Look at the nearest floor lamp. See how wide the base is? See how it rises in the middle? See someone screaming at you for knocking over the nice lamp and breaking the light bulb? See how careful you need to be? Unplug it first.

THE BIG EASY:

What goes under big, upholstered chairs with "skirts" along the bottom? Dustballs, yes. Eyeballs, no. There's usually fabric right under the chair —don't rip it. Instead, tape a film canister inside one of the legs so you can't see the tape or the canister. Leave enough room at the top for easy access to tiny items.

TAKE A MEMO:

Refrigerator doors, family bulletin boards, and message walls are a notorious mess. Hide secret messages on sticky notes **behind** the artwork and phone numbers. Chances are, no one will notice for months.

OH, CHUTE:

If you live in a house with a laundry chute, this quick trick works like a lobster trap. Tape a length of string inside the chute (out of sight) and tape the other end to a zipper-lock bag. Send lightweight items down and haul them back when needed. Or measure the string to stop at the first-floor door, make the drop, then innocently go downstairs and claim your prize. Remember: Dirty clothes will interfere with your dirty work if you dawdle while you dangle.

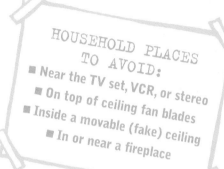

HOUSEHOLD PLACES TO AVOID:
- Near the TV set, VCR, or stereo
- On top of ceiling fan blades
- Inside a movable (fake) ceiling
- In or near a fireplace

CLOTH ENCOUNTERS:

Sometimes families have bedsheets or towels that are old or ugly and never get used. But no one throws them away! Remove the

one on the bottom, fold your cache inside, and delicately put it back in place. This spot might be good for months...unless all your cousins are sleeping over soon! This also works with folded sweaters, especially in the summer.

IN THE KITCHEN:

Almost no place in the kitchen is good for hiding...too many people, too many dangerous items, and someone could get sick or hurt if you ruin their food. The list of things to avoid is very long. Hands off everywhere but these few places:

PROFESSIONAL BOXING:

You can use an **empty** box from cereal, cookies, or packaged foods, once you clean it out. Put your stuff in a plastic bag, and put the box in the back of the cupboard where it belongs. Don't put real food over it, because you'll ruin the food and possibly hurt someone. The box alone should do the job. Expect to get caught when someone gets hungry!

GET MUGGED:

Almost every kitchen has a cupboard filled with coffee mugs. A few in the front get used all the time, and the rest in the back get ignored. Dusty mugs are best. And forget hiding anything here that's dirty or yucky.

FOOD FOR THOUGHT:

On your long list of secret places, the subject of food should definitely be crossed off. Sorry to say, there are just too many risks in hiding things around food, because:

- What you're hiding is probably not clean.
- The act of stashing can ruin the food.
- Food attracts people, so they'll easily discover your cache.
- Food goes bad quickly, attracting bugs and fuzzy mold.
- And most importantly, someone could accidentally eat and choke on whatever you've hidden.

CHEW ON THIS AND HIDE IT ELSEWHERE!

BOWLED OVER:

In the kitchen, you can probably find a fancy big bowl that only sees daylight at dinner parties. Try to figure out how often it's used, and see if you can reach it without breaking either the bowl or your skull. Be picky about what you hide here, since you'll be eating from that bowl one day.

KITCHEN PLACES TO AVOID:

- Near ovens and stoves
- Around electrical appliances
- With anything that could end up in food
- Down the drain
- Near cleaning supplies

BATH TIME:

If you don't think you can find great hiding places in a room with no actual furniture, sit down and think for a minute.

TANKS A LOT:

Here's one of the dumbest places in the house to hide things. Hide something small in an airtight, zipper-lock plastic bag. Tape it behind the toilet. Or **very gently** lift the lid of the toilet's water tank. Tape the bag to the bottom of the lid with masking tape or other strong tape. **Don't let the bag float or it will jam the works!** Also keep in mind that the toilet tank lid is heavy and can break easily— and it's expensive to replace.

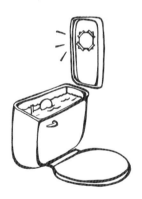

THAT SINKING FEELING:

Lots of bathroom (and kitchen) sinks sit over cupboards. Right over the cupboard doors there's probably a panel that pretends to be a drawer.

It isn't. Tape an envelope behind there for a fast, private hiding place. While you're down there, will it fit behind a pipe? Or along the back wall, up high? **Warning:** There might be dangerous chemicals and cleaners under the sink. Be very careful to remove them and replace them after you're done. Then wash your hands.

BATHROOM QUICKLIST:

If it's small and you can roll it up tight, try these bathroom hides:

- In a travel toothbrush holder
- Rolled up inside a toilet-paper roll
- In an innocent-looking box in the back of a cabinet
- Taped to the back of the sink
- Between the bath mat and the tub
- Behind the curtains, hanging at the top

WARNING: STAY OUT OF THE PLUMBING, THE DRAINS, THE FAN, THE MEDICINE CABINET, AND ANYTHING PEOPLE USE ON THEIR BODIES.

BASEMENTS, ATTICS, GARAGES, & CATCH-ALL CLOSETS:

If something seems boring and useful, you probably don't want to know what happens when it breaks. (Is that a sewer pipe or a poisonous gas pipe? Hmmm...) Don't mess with smelly, sharp, or mechanical items, either, like lawn mowers or furnaces. It's too easy to make a dumb move that will cost a lot of money... or hurt someone. Be smart.

HERE'S WHERE THE REAL SPIES WOULD HIDE IT:

■ In an empty box that came with something that's in use, like an answering machine or waffle iron ■ Under the holiday decorations (during the rest of the year) ■ Under the summer items in winter ■ Under the winter items in summer ■ Mixed in with a boring box full of papers ■ Inside a broken (but safe) household item—like an old vacuum cleaner or sewing machine ■ At the bottom of a travel toiletry kit

old Income tax papers

Great Outdoor Hiding Places

**Outdoor hiders have lots of places to hide.
And lots of issues to think about. Do you want to hide it
for a long time...or for just a few hours?
Are other people likely to come poking around? Will the
weather be a factor? Ponder before placement.**

NEAR HOME:

TRICKY TRASH:

You think trash is disgusting? So does everyone
else. If you're clever, you can hide your goodies in
any kind of box or bag that **looks** like trash. Then
put it where trash goes—under your family's trash
can, or close enough. Trash is so safe you could hide
diamonds in it, but stick to the trash you know.
Also, don't expect your trash cache to stick around
after garbage day...this is a **very** short-term hide.

CONSTRUCTION OBSTRUCTION:

Somewhere near home, somebody's building something, fixing something, or tearing something up. Chances are they probably left some materials here and there in temporary piles. That's right: **temporary.** Bricks, rocks, lumber, and other building supplies have more important things to do besides hiding your stuff. So be careful **and** quick.

TOOL TIME:

If your local adult has outdoor storage for tools and equipment, you might be the only person who ever goes in there. Avoid the sharp stuff.

THE FENCE SITTER:

Lots of metal gates and fences are made with hollow poles. Is there a low fence near you to examine? Sometimes there are little caps on top of each pole. If one is loose, you have a long, deep hiding place of your very own. You can tie a wire to the top and dangle your cache down inside it. Or put it in a plastic bag that's big enough to keep your goodies from sliding down too far.

HOSE HOLDER:

Some families leave their garden hoses outside. Is yours wrapped up in a circle? (Hiding place!) Is yours coiled around a little ferris wheel? (Hiding place!) Does yours lie in the plants like a snake? Tape your treasure right to it, or connect a string between the hose and your cache—then plant it among the plants.

GNOME HOME:

Nobody understands where lawn gnomes come from. Their popularity is a complete mystery. Same with little statues, windmills, even flamingos. If this sounds like a lawn near you, give the lawn ornament a quiet look. Don't knock anything over or force it...just see if there's a good little hiding place somewhere. That's one friend who'll always keep your secret.

39

OUT & ABOUT:

SLIDE IT BY THEM:

Playgrounds in general are lousy places to hide stuff. All you've got are kids and custodians—the two groups most likely to find what you hide. In the entire playground, what's the most dependable place for a short-term hide? Under the slide. Don't bury it; you won't fit and it takes too long. Just wrap it in something dark and waterproof, near the bottom.

SNOW JOB:

Some ideas only work sometimes in some places. Keyword: snow. Make a snowman and give it a secret stomach. Set up a snow fort with its own hidden mailbox. Take a boring little snow pile and bury a boring little trash bag. The usual warnings apply: Snow melts, piles shift, people shovel, objects freeze. But why let that stop you?

BUSHWHACKING:

What's that under the bush? Leaves? Branches? Pine needles? Sounds good. And the only people under there are squirrels, who aren't really people. Lay flat items under a natural cover for a short-term hide. Or dig a hole small enough to hide a washed-out yogurt container. Then give your cache a blanket of brush to hide it a while longer.

LOG ON:

Fallen logs, tree stumps, wooden guard rails—what do they all have in common? They were once trees. And trees are very polite about rotting and making nice holes for hiding. Wrap your cache in a plastic bag for a short-term hide. If you're lucky enough to have nature nearby, pick a low-lying log near a path. You can hollow out a hole for a long-term vault that would make any beaver proud.

DON'T POO-POO THIS IDEA:

Go to a novelty store. Buy a fake doggy poo for a few dollars. Make sure it's hollow on the inside. This is a brilliant place to leave something small outside, like a house key. No one, not even a dog, would bother checking this out.

EXCELLENT SIGNS:

Quick Quiz #1: Name three neighborhoods where there are absolutely no signs posted anywhere. Guess what? You don't live in any of them.
Quick Quiz #2: How many signs have you really examined closely for hiding places? Guess what? Tape, magnets, sticky notes, or your own homemade solution will help any sign keep your secret.

BENCH, BUS, & BEYOND:

Park benches, bus shelters, and community message boards are meant for everyone to use, but not always for the same reasons. You can leave messages on, around, or underneath them—and your friends can come by later to collect. Be careful of sharp objects, strange smells, or people who might be hanging around. Use your head.

OUTDOOR ADVENTURE SURVIVAL KIT:
Here's what not to do outside.

- DON'T bother people's yards, gardens, lawns, and landscaping. People are incredibly picky, they'll find what you hide, and they'll get mad.

- DON'T do permanent damage. Do you really want to spend your next three years' allowance on tulip bulbs?

- DON'T play around pipes, wires, and anything else like that. Once you break it, you'll find out only too quickly why it was there. If you live.

- DON'T do daredevil things on ladders, in trees, near water, in traffic, and so on. If you need a book to explain how **not** to kill yourself, you shouldn't be reading this one. Got it?

School Secrets

The second and third reasons for hiding things at school are to pass messages and to protect your stuff. (The first reason is to have fun, but you already knew that.) These educational clues will help you hide almost anything...except your report card.

SETTING UP YOUR LOCKER:

On the outside, your locker looks just like everyone else's. But what is different on the inside? Maybe yours has a few little secrets of its own...

HIDE IN PLAIN SIGHT:

Even the smallest little corners, folds, and turns can make your locker a private vault. Open your eyes and take a look around. Are there parts that are hard to see, unless you're very short or very tall? What color is the paint? Will magnets stick to it? Does the "ceiling" go higher than the door? If you said yes to any of these, you're in luck.

MAGNETIC ATTRACTION:

Get a magnetic "hide-a-key" holder at a hardware store for a dollar or two. Or get a magnet and glue it to a low, flat, small box. Cover the box in black tape if it's another color. Put the magnetic box under your locker shelf, in a corner, or anywhere it won't be seen, to hide money and more.

STICKY PENS & PENCILS:

Before opening your locker, roll up a bit of masking tape or adhesive tape around a pen, **sticky side out.** With the clip side down, reach up under the shelf to hide your pen behind the lip of the shelf, if there is one. Or maybe your locker hangs over the wall a little bit at the bottom. This is another good place to tape up a pen or pencil—you can pretend to be tying your shoes!

QUICK PENCIL DROP:

Get a dark-colored travel toothbrush holder. Tape it into a dark corner of your locker. (That may be the corner closest to your lock, or the hinges. Look around from the usual angles.) You can store your pens and pencils in this handy holster at the end of every day... out of sight.

ARTFUL ART:

Here's a smaller version of the Perfect Poster (page 78). Glue a picture or poster to a piece of cardboard or poster board. (It should be at least an inch narrower than the locker wall.) Glue small, thin magnets to each corner, almost to the edges, but not exactly. Glue or tape a pocket, an open envelope, or trading-card sleeves to the back of the cardboard. Now you have a removable place to hide your cards, notes, and papers.

FLIP ART:

This idea is a little simpler than the last one. Glue the same poster to the same cardboard. But tape it along the top edge only. Tape an open envelope or anything else to the wall, not the poster. Just flip it up when you want your cache. Make sure no one's watching!

FLOOR BOARD OF EDUCATION:

Make a fake floor for your locker that can hide a few comics, cards, or bad test papers! Measure the real floor with a larger piece of paper or newspaper. Crease the edges along each side to get an exact measure. At home, use the creased paper as an outline to trace over a piece of cardboard. Cut it out with scissors. Use paint, construction paper, or contact paper, so your fake floor matches the locker's color. (Or you can always use black.)

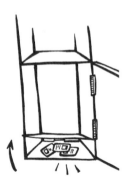

At your locker, make a trapdoor hinge like this: Put the fake floor in place. Then lift the front like you're opening the hood of a car. When the fake floor is against the back wall, use strips of masking tape to connect the fake floor to the real one. When you lower the floor, the tape should be completely hidden underneath. Don't hide too much under your fake floor—it'll get found. This idea also works for making a fake ceiling, holding it up with magnets or tape.

FROM DESK TO DOOR:

Some secret hiding places have a lot of class. So it's a good thing you're in class a lot, too. Right? Here are a few cool school ideas you can really learn, if you do your homework.

THE WRITE STUFF:

Need a simple under-the-desk pencil holster? Of course you do. Roll a three-inch-long piece of masking tape around and around your pencil, 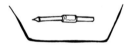 **sticky side out.** Then put the pencil under your desk or table where your hand would naturally go. Pull out the pen and leave the tape tube stuck to the bottom. Because the inside is not sticky, the pencil goes in and out easily. Bet this works for pens, too.

TRUE OR FALSE?

If your desk can hold books inside, you can adapt a few locker tricks for fun and security. Put in a false bottom or fake art. You can tape an envelope underneath for holding important papers during the day. Keep it light so nothing falls out.

BULLETIN BORED?

Keep papers safe during the day by tacking an envelope **behind** bulletins, or posters, or anything you can easily pull away and put back. This can be tricky in a room full of eyes, so make sure you know what you want to do. And do it quickly.

CLIP TIP:

Have you ever seen a magnetic clip? It's a pretty strong clip connected to a pretty strong magnet, about an inch long. One clip could certainly hold a comic book, pad, or pen behind a file cabinet or under a cold radiator. Find them in the store next to thumbtacks and paper clips.

FORTUNE COOKIE:

If you've got a dollar to hide, a phone number to hold, or a note you have to have, the answer might be right in your pocket. Take a pen that unscrews and unscrew it.

Roll up your piece of paper **super tight** around the ink cartridge. You might need a piece of tape to keep it rolled up. If you haven't been too ambitious, you should be able to rescrew the top and click the pen. Also a great way to pass notes. Speaking of which...

PASSING MESSAGES:

Passing messages takes planning, timing, and keeping cool. When it works, it's no accident. And if you get caught, it's not our fault and we don't know you.

CLEVER CLUES:

You can hide your message and leave your partner clues for the pickup. If it's under a water fountain at school, on the second floor by the music room, your clue can be "H_2O on 2 near tunes." Leave this message in your partner's drop place. Don't make it impossible to figure out.

A NOTE IN PASSING

KNOW THE PLACE: You and your partner should agree in advance where to make the drop.

KNOW THE PLAN: Will it be a one-way or round-trip drop? Will your partner leave a reply for you at the same drop place? Sometimes each of you needs to have your own secret location.

KNOW THE TIMING: When will it be there? Agree in advance, or else one of you will come up empty. It's suspicious to visit a drop place more often than necessary.

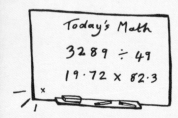

Today's Math
$3289 \div 49$
19.72×82.3

KNOW THE SIGNAL: If you haven't planned a drop but you need to get a message out, here's how to do it. Arrange a signal that your partner will find, like an innocent message on a locker door, or a secret symbol on the classroom board. Your partner should then know where to go for the real message.

KNOW THE RISKS: Even the best-hidden messages should still be in code. Expect that your message will be found by the worst possible person. Not only that, codes make even the dullest message more fun.

PICK A PROPER PLACE: Here's how to find an unfindable drop place. What works best?

- Choose a public place so you can explain why you're there. No trespassing!
- Start your search along walls and edges, not necessarily in the middle of a place.
- Look up, down, and sideways...in places where people don't normally focus.
- Make sure your drop place isn't about to be carried away, cleaned up, or carted into a closet.

STICK WITH A WINNER:

Leaving secret messages doesn't give you lots of free time. You want to get in and out fast. The most sensible message system is the sticky note. They're not expensive, they come in all kinds of sizes and colors, you get lots on a pad, and they're fast. Each partner can pick a signature color.

POSTER POSER:

Now and then, posters pop up for bake sales, school plays, and special visitors. One might make a good message drop. Peel the tape away from the bottom, stow your sticky note, and put the poster back in place.

SPECIAL BULLETIN:

School bulletin boards can be perfect places for short-term message drops. Flat items can be taped or tacked behind official papers. Don't damage any public messages or message boards while you're setting up your own.

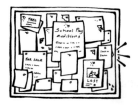

BACK IT UP:

For extra security, write your coded message on the **back** of the sticky note, and write something really plain and boring on the front, like "Field trip on Monday."

CODE WARRIOR:

Elite intelligence operators know two or three codes. If one gets broken, there's always a fallback. If it isn't obvious to your partner, use a special symbol to explain which code is in use.

FOUNTAIN OF KNOWLEDGE:

You probably can't remember the last time you looked under a water fountain. Neither can anyone else. That's why this is a great place to leave secret messages between classes.

IN A BIND:

If you're like most students, you probably don't value your textbooks. Look again. Open one on a desk and the binding makes a handy opening. Voilà! A great place to store notes.

MOUSEPAD NOTEPAD:

Next time you see a mouse in school, you're seeing a great short-term message drop. Leave it under the mousepad, or under the keyboard, just before your friend comes by. Watch for watching eyes.

FAST WIPE:

What's that in back of the napkin dispenser? Not napkins. It's a nice little bit of space to leave a note for someone. But plan a quick pickup...cafeteria workers move fast.

SECRET BOOKMARK:

Pick a book, any book, as a drop place. Agree on a permanent page number—say, page 31. Leave a small note, not something huge.

PRIVATE DICTIONARY:

Here's a game the spies play while waiting for their submarine. Pick a mystery word in a dictionary. At that word's page, slip in a little note with the secret name of a drop place. Then give your partner a clue to the mystery word. Make it a fun clue, but not too hard to figure out. When your partner gets the clue,  a reward can be waiting at the drop place you named in the note. And then it's your turn to figure out the next clue... You can try this with other kinds of books, too.

TEACHER'S A HELPER:

Aim low and outside, right on the bottom of the teacher's desk. Who looks under there? Few custodians, and certainly no teachers! Walk by, stop, pop your sticky-taped or magnetic hiding system into place, and keep moving. Getting your stuff back should be done just as smoothly. Pretending to tie your shoes is a good excuse. Just not too often.

make your own Secret Vaults

Up to now, you've been learning the science of finding hiding places. Now it's time to explore the art of making them. Build each of these homemade vaults, then think up your own. They'll work while you play.

THE TRAPDOOR BOX:

Here's a simply deceptive vault that's easy to make and easy to ignore. Hides papers, comics, cards, and other flat items up to 1 inch high.

MAKING IT:

1. Pick a **cardboard box** or **shoebox** that looks plain and boring.

2. Get a **second box** of the same color and material. One side of this box will be cut up to make the false bottom of the vault box. Make sure it's big enough, and doesn't have holes.

3. Measure the bottom of the vault box with some **newspaper**. Spread it out and crease the paper's edges to make an accurate impression.

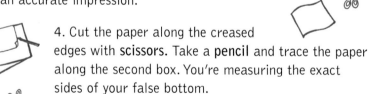

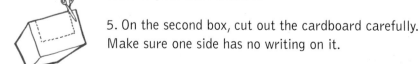

4. Cut the paper along the creased edges with **scissors.** Take a **pencil** and trace the paper along the second box. You're measuring the exact sides of your false bottom.

5. On the second box, cut out the cardboard carefully. Make sure one side has no writing on it.

HIDING IT:

1. Lay your treasure flat. Comics, cards, etc. should be in tight plastic bags. Tape down each bag to make sure nothing will slide around. Help the new bottom sit evenly—fold up **extra cardboard** to fill in big gaps. Don't hide so much that the bottom looks fake!

2. Keeping your hands at the edges, push in the false bottom. Don't rush it, since air has to come out. When the false bottom lays flat, fill it with things that won't crush your treasure. Then leave your vault in a corner or a closet. Put stuff on it and around it, and make it look ignored.

OPENING IT:

Remove the stuff on top of the vault. Turn the box over. The bottom should slide down. If it's tight, take a **butter knife** and gently pry out the edges of the false bottom. Make sure you don't pull too hard and dent the false bottom. Don't give away clues!

THE HOLLOW BOOK:

Here's a long-term hiding place that's worth reading about. And it will cover your stuff perfectly! Hides anything that's the size of a cassette tape box, or smaller.

MAKING IT:

This project needs an adult's permission and help with the cutting.

1. Select a book. Don't wreck a book that someone might want to read. Go to a used bookstore and find a **big, cheap, old hardcover book**. Or ask for a damaged book you can have for free. Pick a boring book that won't attract readers. Suggested titles: 1953 Travel Guide to Bolivia, You Can Be a Blacksmith, Why I Yodel, and Introducing Television: It's Radio with Pictures. Or use an old phone book.

2. You want a sturdy book, so don't cut too big a hole. First you need to make a pattern. Cut a rectangular piece of **cardboard** that leaves a few inches on each side. If the book is big enough, use a **videotape** box as a guide. If your book is smaller, use a **music tape box.**

3. Leave several pages at the beginning of the book to hide your hole. Then fit the **rectangular pattern** on the page where your hole begins. Use a **pencil** to trace the pattern. Now you can go in two directions.

THE FAST & SIMPLE WAY:

4a. This version is quick to make, but leaves a hole at the top of every page. (Put it on a high shelf and no one will see the hole.) Trace your pattern along the top edge of each page. Leave enough room on the sides and bottom to support your cache without the book

63

falling apart. Now take **scissors** and cut around the pattern, starting at the top.

5a. On the next page, you can use the hole you just cut for your outline. Snip each page using the previous page as a guide. Go almost to the book's last page... you want to leave several pages in the back for support and secrecy.

THE SLOW & SECRET WAY:

4b. This version takes longer to make because you can't see the hole from the outside. As before, draw the rectangular outline, but in the middle. Leave at least an inch on each side. Now ask an adult to poke one sharp point of the scissors into a corner of the outline. Once the scissors go through the page, cut the center out normally.

5b. Take a ballpoint pen and trace the cut-out page on the one beneath it. Repeat this on each page until you're most of the way through the book. Be sure to leave several pages uncut at the end for extra support.

HIDING IT:

1. You may want to tape the inside pages of your book together so nothing falls out. That's okay, but put the tape INSIDE THE HOLE ONLY, along the cut-out edges, like making walls for a swimming pool. Don't stick tape between pages. You can see it from the outside, and it will become a bookmark that opens right to your secret hole. Not so secret!

2. Whatever you hide should sit right in the hole, and not bulge. If you used a tape box for a pattern, try tucking the box inside the book for extra protection. Then put your secret book up on a shelf next to other books you don't read often.

THE EMPTY BOOM BOX:

This vault may take a bit more work, but it's worth the effort and fools basically everybody. Get permission, and don't break anything that still works. It will hide whatever will fit inside!

MAKING IT:

1. Make sure the **boom box** you're going to use is already broken. If you don't have an old one, go to an electronics repair shop and ask if they have a broken one you can have. If they won't give one away, maybe you can buy one for a few dollars. These instructions work for a broken **VCR** as well.

2. Disconnect the **electrical cord** and throw it away. You DO NOT want to even THINK about electricity near your vault.

3. Take a **screwdriver** and remove the screws that hold the case together. Pull the two halves apart. Don't remove screws on the handle unless it's the only way to open the case. Put these screws in a special place for safekeeping.

4. Almost every boom box is made the same way—the insides are really one piece. These guts stay in place with just a few screws, so all the machinery pulls out easily. Finding the screws isn't hard. They're usually at the edges, and sometimes in the middle of the case. Unscrew any screws you want, then give the entire inside a pull. Eventually, it will budge!

5. Speaker wires may need to be cut with **scissors** or **wire cutters**.
Though you can pull out parts without fear (and with fun), be careful of
the cassette tape door—you don't want it to fall off!

HIDING IT:

Once the case is hollow, you can cover any inside edges with **masking
tape**, if they seem sharp. Fit your secret cache inside any way you want.
If you wrap it, it won't rattle when it moves. Put the cover back on and
use the screws you put aside. Move your vault somewhere you would
usually put a broken boom box, like a closet floor or under the bed...
and forget about it!

THE LUMPY PILLOW:

You can rest assured you'll always be comfortable using this secret vault. Hides solid objects of any size, depending on your pillow.

MAKING IT:

1. It all begins by choosing a **stiff but spongy pillow** that most people have on a couch. NOT a bed pillow. Does yours match these critical requirements?

- It's filled only with foam. No feathers!
- It's got a zipper for easy access.
- It's not incredibly ugly or smelly, so nobody throws it away one day.
- It's not incredibly nice, so nobody cares if you use it. Get permission.
- It's not incredibly expensive, not worth more than a few dollars.

2. Open the zipper and take out the piece of **foam**. You may have to scrunch it in the middle to get it out.

3. Look at your foam. You're going to hollow out the middle, then cover the hole with some of the foam. Use your hands to pluck out little pieces of foam. Don't pull out too much foam, or the pillow won't fool anyone.

4. Stop plucking when your hole is a good size and there's still enough foam around the edges to feel like a normal pillow.

HIDING IT:

1. Put your cache inside, maybe wrapped in a **sock, washcloth,** or **little towel** to keep it soft. Make sure there's room to put some of the foam back on top.

2. Choose a few foam pieces you took out. Tape them together from the **inside** to make a plug for the top of the hole. You want to feel foam on the outside — not tape. Put in the plug.

3. Put your pillow back into its case. Zip the zipper and toss it casually on the bed, or put it in a corner, or stick it in the closet. You don't want other people sleeping on it. As with any pillow, use your head.

THE VIDEO VAULT:

This little vault is a real star—it's compact, it's fast, and it's super-easy to ignore. Action! Hides anything that fits inside a videotape box—about the size of a small paperback book.

MAKING IT:

1. Pick a jammed or broken **videotape.** Or pick a bad video that's worth the sacrifice. If it's not yours, get permission. And make sure it's the kind of videotape that's held together with screws.

2. Open the plastic case with a **little screwdriver** and save the screws. Then turn the case over.

3. Remove the cover. See the little piece of plastic that covers the tape? Look for a square button in

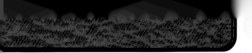

the corner to push. Push it. Now you can get to the tape. Take out all the contents.

4. Take some **black construction paper** or **black electrical tape.** Put it **on the inside** of the clear plastic window (if there is one) to hide your stuff from view. Or if you have a sticker that can cover the window from the outside, write the name of your "movie" on it.

HIDING IT:

Tuck your cache inside the black tape box. Tape it down or use stuffing so that nothing shakes around. Try not to make it too heavy or it'll feel fake. Put the screws back in. Then put it back into its **printed box** and bury it on the boring end of your video pile. Don't make it a good movie! Make up dumb movie titles like Windmills of Miniature Golf, The Hog Farmer, or Stronger Elbows in 30 Days! You can even write "Broken" on it somewhere. Definitely DON'T put this in your VCR, or that's what will be broken.

THE SECRET WALL:

This is one of the harder vaults to discover, because it's not simple to open. Use it for things you won't need often. Great for hiding books, papers, comics, cards, and items up to a few inches thick.

MAKING IT:

1. Find a closet with built-in shelves, a low kitchen cupboard, or shelves behind a door. Pick a low shelf, if you can, because people are less likely to see the wall behind it when they're standing up.

2. Get material to use for your back wall. You can cut a piece of **cardboard** from a large box. You can use a light, stiff material called **Foamcore**, which is sold in art stores. You can work with an adult to

cut a piece of **plywood** to fit your space. Or find
another flat material that's bigger than the wall
you're hiding, and that you can cut.

3. Measure the four sides of the back wall with
some **newspaper.** Spread it out and crease the
paper's edges along each side. Pull out the newspaper and cut it along
the creased edges with **scissors.**

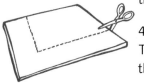

4. Place the newspaper on your wall material.
Trace around the edges with a **pencil** to measure
the wall.

5. If you can't safely cut your fake wall with scissors, ask an adult to
help you.

6. Make sure your wall is the right color. Use **paint,** or cover it with **paper,**
or stretch **cloth** across it so it isn't noticeable. **Contact paper** (sticky shelf
paper) comes in lots of colors and even in wood-grain patterns.

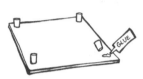

7. Take four empty **thread spools,** or empty **plastic film canisters,** or something else about an inch deep. Glue them just inside each of the four corners of your fake wall, but not all the way to the corners.

8. Cut a piece of **fishing line** or **string** that's about six inches longer than the bottom of your wall. Tie small loops at each end—you'll pull these to open the wall. Glue or

tape the line near the inside bottom edge, so that you can easily pull out your wall once it's in place. You can also run it toward the top if that's more hidden.

HIDING IT:

Stand your treasure up against the back wall. Think about using an envelope or bag to hold it in place, maybe even attach it to the real wall. Put your fake wall gently in place—making sure

the loops are on the outside. Then put extra stuff in front to hide it!

OPENING IT:

Just pull both secret string loops at the same time. Once the wall starts to come away, you can just use your hands.

VALID VAULT ADVICE:

As much as you might want to pry open, pull apart, and puncture everything in your house, don't.

Most people prefer a world where their books don't have holes, their pillows are still stuffed, and their boom boxes can actually play music. Use your own stuff to hide your own stuff, or it's you who will be hidden away for a **very** long time.

THE PERFECT POSTER:

If you need to get to trading cards often, this is a quick vault that's really a piece of art. Hides trading cards, secret maps, letters.

MAKING IT:

1. Many posters are mounted on stiff poster board or cardboard. If your **poster** isn't mounted yet, you need to measure its edges with a **ruler.** You can buy the right-sized **poster board** to mount it on, or you can cut out a piece of large **cardboard** to fit. Then tape, glue, or staple the poster onto the board.

2. Some mounted posters come with string or wire to hang on the wall. If yours doesn't, or you've just mounted it, measure a piece of string or

fishing line an inch wider than your poster. Tape or glue each end to the poster backing, not far from the top, and make it strong enough to hold the weight of the poster and what it's mounted to. Get permission to put a nail or pushpin in the wall at the right height. When it's in place, hang the poster from the string. It should be easy to put on and take off.

HIDING IT:

Tape or glue trading-card sleeves or comic-book bags onto the poster backing. You can also use envelopes or make thin pockets out of folded paper and fasten them on. Make sure the secret bags and pockets stay hidden—don't let them come close to the edge. A few inches inside is best. And don't make it too thick, either. When you turn your poster around, you can look at dozens of cards all at the same time!

THAT WEIRD THING AT THE JUNK SALE:

What else makes a perfect vault? Keep your eyes open...you never know what you're going to find. Clever minds invent clever vaults.

WHAT TO LOOK FOR:

Garage sales, tag sales, used furniture stores, junk stores, and the Salvation Army store are excellent places for your search. Here's what makes the ideal vault:

1. **It's the right size.** Keep in mind what you're hiding. Will it fit? And will it fit easily in your room? Where are you going to put it? Know before you decide.

2. **It's made for hiding.** Remember that your vault has to be easy to take apart and easy to put together again. Check to see that it isn't fragile. Be very sure it has no dangerous parts or edges that can hurt you.

3. **It's not too grungy.** Kids are famous for getting attached to smelly, dirty, mangy things. Maybe it will hide all your trading cards perfectly, but if it attracts bugs (or wrinkled noses), it will soon attract the garbage truck. And then where will your trading cards be?

4. **It's the right price.** As a rule, the best vaults come from the best bargains. You can hide it in a boring, cheap shoebox as easily as in a 1,000-year-old suit of armor. But which one will people examine first?

5. **It's not too weird.** An old bucket lamp without a cord, or an empty fire extinguisher without a bottom, or a big hollow toy or game make excellent starting points. Also, they make sense in your room. On the other hand, a broken refrigerator, an oil drum, or a car engine are most likely more hassle than they're worth. Imagination keeps you ahead of the game, and permission keeps you in the game. It's best to have both.

Map It & Find It

Indoors and outdoors...underground and above...if you forget where you hid it, you'll be looking high and low.

MAKING AN INDOOR MAP:

As best as you can, draw the outline of the room where you've hidden your treasure. It doesn't have to be perfect, just close.

For each major piece of furniture in the room, draw a basic shape. Chairs and some tables can be squares. Beds, couches, and other tables can be rectangles. Some things might even be round. You don't have to draw every piece—just the big ones, and also any piece that's connected to a hiding place. If a hiding place is not connected to furniture, use a different shape, like a triangle for a wall location or a star if it's on the floor.

Use symbols or colors to mark what's hiding and what isn't. Your favorite color or two can be used where you've hidden something. Colors you don't like so much can mean there's nothing there. Try using different patterns to mean "something's here" or "nothing doing."

Now that you have your basic room map, it's time to get creative.

A BEAST OF A MAP:

Instead of drawing the basic shapes, draw a completely original picture. Let's say you're drawing animals. Snakes can be the chairs. An elephant can be the bed. And so on. Now you have a room full of critters. Use colors, patterns, or other decorations to show which animals are hiding something. Or maybe ALL the horses are hiding places and every other animal is a decoy. Someone looking at your picture will only see a lot of animals.

What room is it? Use clues in the name of your "picture." Sleepy Animals can mean your bedroom. Animals on TV can mean the room with the TV.

PICTURE THIS:

The animal-map idea also works with other figures. Make aliens. Make a town. Make a dinosaur pit. Make a race car track. Make doodles that don't look much like anything...but they all show what's in a room.

MAKING A WORD MAP:

Take three pieces of paper. On the first piece, write the word WHAT at the top. Make a list of the things you've hidden. Give each type of thing its own number.

On the second piece, write the word WHERE at the top. List each hiding place, and give each place its own letter.

Here's an example of a word map:

WHAT
1. Comic books
2. Joke books
3. Trading cards
4. Video games
5. Dollar bills

WHERE
A. Trapdoor box
B. Photo album
C. Dictionary pages
D. Under bottom dresser drawer

Now make your linking page, called a NEXUS. It's your third piece of paper, and it lists your actual hides, like this:

NEXUS
1A   2A   3B   4A   5C   5D

This means you've got comics, joke books, and video games in your trapdoor box vault. Trading cards are hidden in your photo album, and dollars are stashed in the dictionary pages and under the dresser drawer. Simple! You can also share a version of this map system with a friend at school.

SPECIAL MAP HIDING PLACES:

Hide each of your three important word-map pages in **separate places** that are only for maps. Now all you have to remember is three hiding places. Remember to update your NEXUS whenever you add or move things. If anyone finds one of the pages, it's meaningless. But be the most careful with the WHERE list of hiding places. You might want to write it in code.

TREASURE MAPS:

Make a map to remember exactly where you've hidden things. You can also use a map to challenge your friends to find what you've hidden!

REFERENCE POINTS:

A functional treasure map will tell you two things: the general area and local landmarks.

THE GENERAL AREA:

Pick a place that's familiar and accessible—Kevin's backyard, the basement, the playground. This gives you a starting point but doesn't tell you a lot. You can describe places with clues that only you would know.

LOCAL LANDMARKS:

Now you can begin to give specific clues. Each landmark is something that's easy to identify, doesn't move, or isn't likely to be moved. The route you describe should also be clear and straight. The last item you describe should be your final landmark.

If you're in Merle's backyard, your landmarks might be listed like this:
1. Stand directly between the shed and the water faucet.
2. Walk five feet toward the house and stop. Look up.

3. Follow the path of the large tree branch you're under until you can see the Spanglers' kitchen window.

4. Look under the closest flowerpot. (This flowerpot will be your final landmark.)

HIDE & GO SEEK:

Mapping has other uses as well. Using local landmarks and final landmarks, you can create an entire scavenger hunt for your friends. Once they find where you've sent them, give them a clue that sends them off in another direction. This game works both indoors and outdoors.

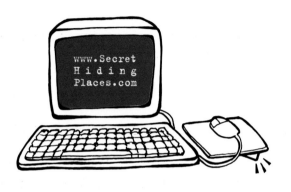

www.Secret
Hiding
Places.com

SO SECRET IT'S NOT IN THIS BOOK

There are two kinds of secrets: regular secrets and secret secrets. Guess which ones we're talking about now? And guess where they are?

WE HID THEM.

"No fair!" you say. "Top secret!" we say. If you really want to find them, you need to get on the Internet:

www.SecretHidingPlaces.com

And keep this book handy, because each password is buried inside it.

Let's say you get past security. Now you'll have top clearance to new places for hiding stuff around the house, outdoors, and at school. Sometimes we'll add new ones, too. So watch out.

You can also email your own favorite hiding places for our next book. Each suggestion we use gets you a free copy of that book, and we'll even add your name, if you want!

Remember, only people who own this book can unlock the secret secrets. Isn't that clever of us?

HOW SECRET IS YOUR SECRET?

Ask yourself these very important questions:

Is the place RIGHT for what you're hiding?

Is it a hiding place you'll need often, or just sometimes?

When are other people likely to visit the site?

Is it a place that could be changed or moved by other people?

Does it look **too much** like a hiding place, where others might look?

Can you make the place look natural and unsuspicious without much work?

Does the site work on its own, or do you need to add something?

Can you get in and out without attracting attention?

Are there some things that won't hide well in that place?

If the place is outdoors, also think about this:

Are weather conditions or other elements likely to interfere?

Can you get to your site all year round?

Can the site be easily mapped?

HOW TO HIDE THIS BOOK:

The experts agree! **Secret Hiding Places** is a treasure chest of great ideas for clever minds. And like all treasure, this book has to be buried. Not in the yard or under third base, but somewhere handy, in plain sight, where nobody will find it.

The next page may look strange, but it's useful. Those are fake sides for CDs. Just cut them out and tape them around the book's spine. Presto! It vanishes when you hide it with other CDs. (Maybe that's why the book's shaped this way!)

To make your own full, fake cover, measure the book cover for a perfect fit, and leave a little extra room at each edge so your fake cover can be taped to the real one, on the inside. You can also tape a real CD cover to this one. Or just hide it in any of the great secret places you learned about in this book. But use a map to remember where you stowed it...

HAPPY HIDING!

Miriam and Leah Sing Whale Songs   Vol. 5   CD508522

The Sound of Teakettles   CD5440

The Hydrants   Just Say no to Dogs   CD24256

Snore: Music that Makes Adults Sleep Like Babies   CD444742

Droolbucket   Sophie, So Good   CD032699

Jesse A. Mouse   Haydn Goes "EEK!"   CD4821846